ANATOMY Coloring Book

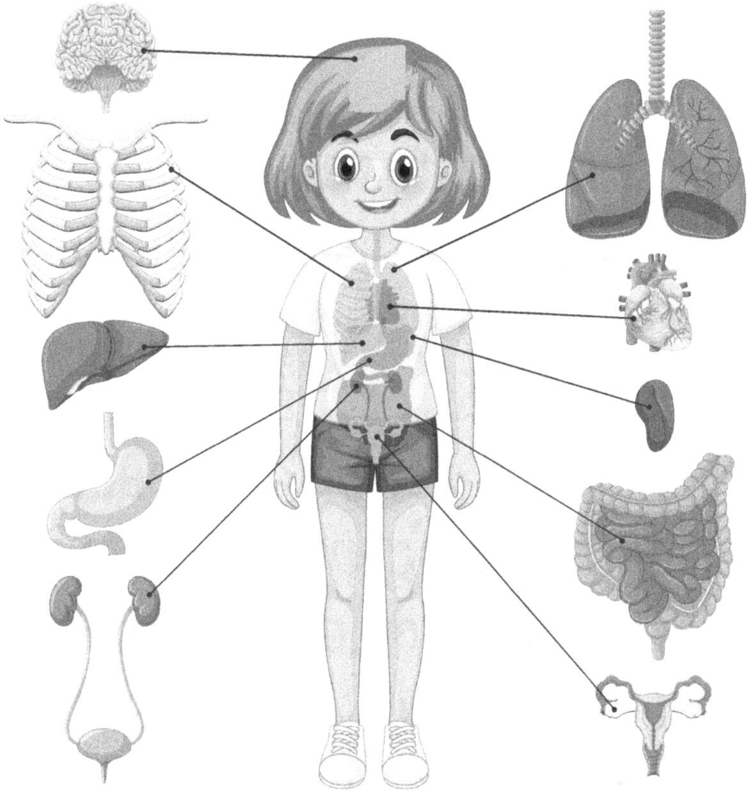

This Book Belongs To

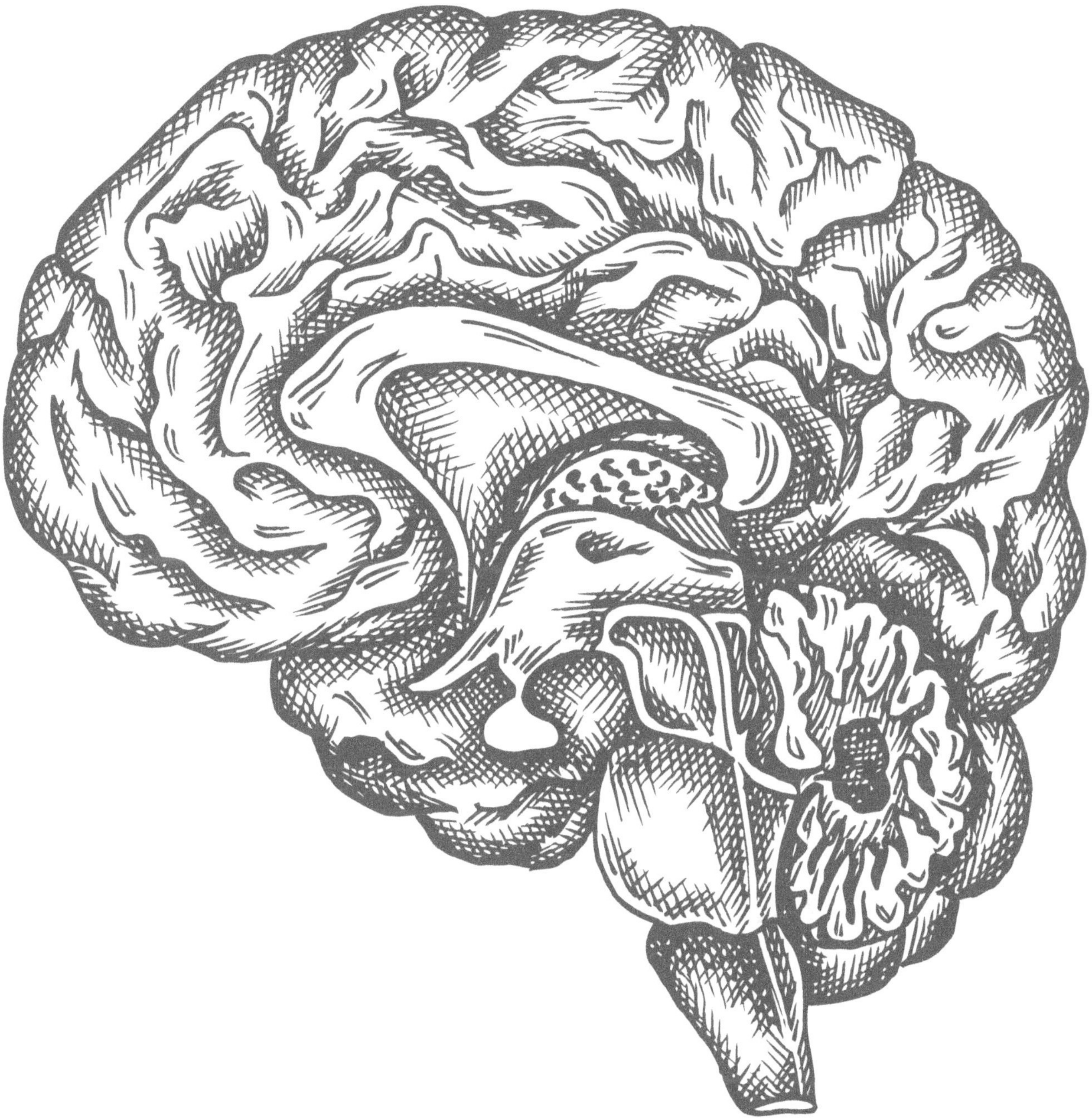

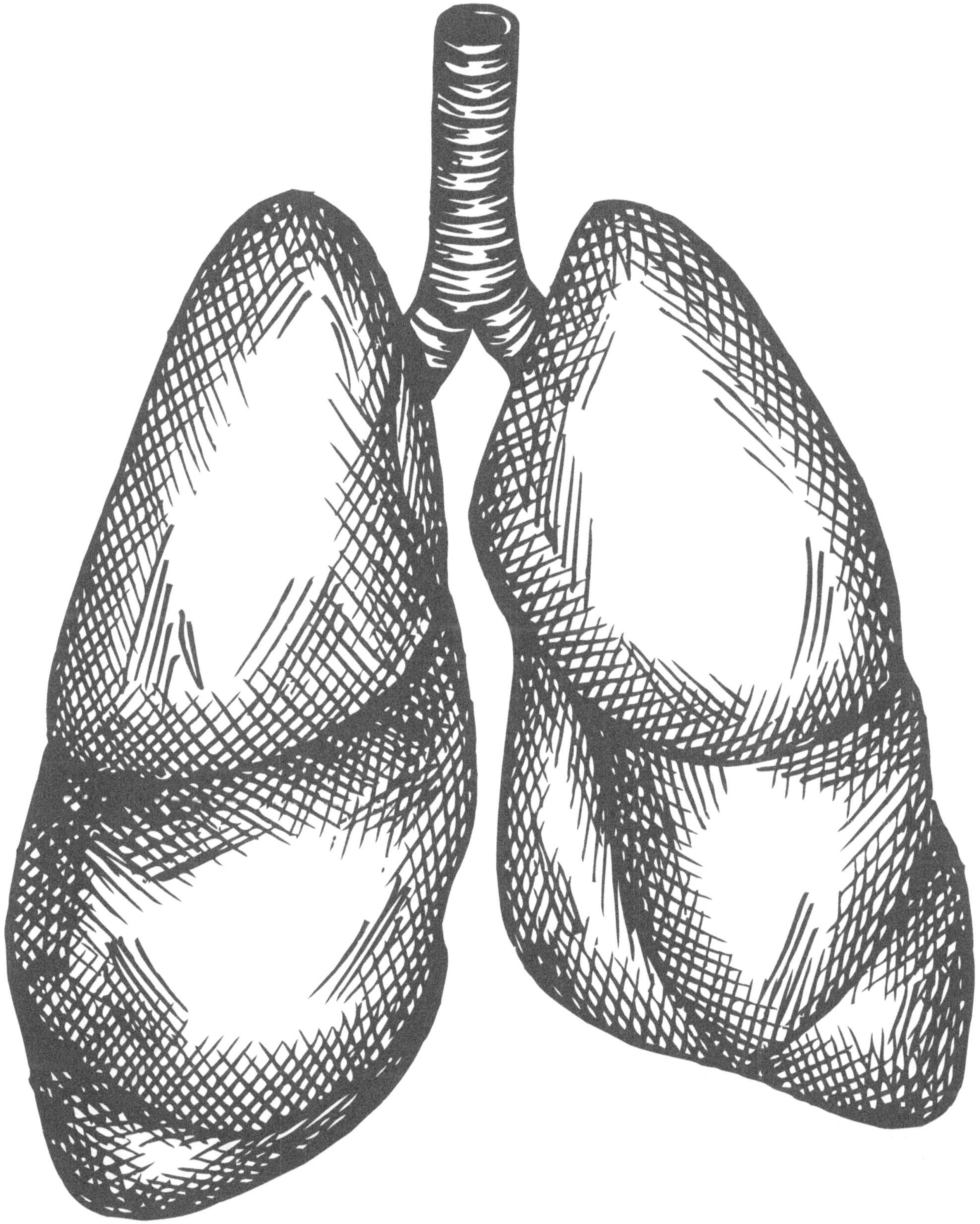

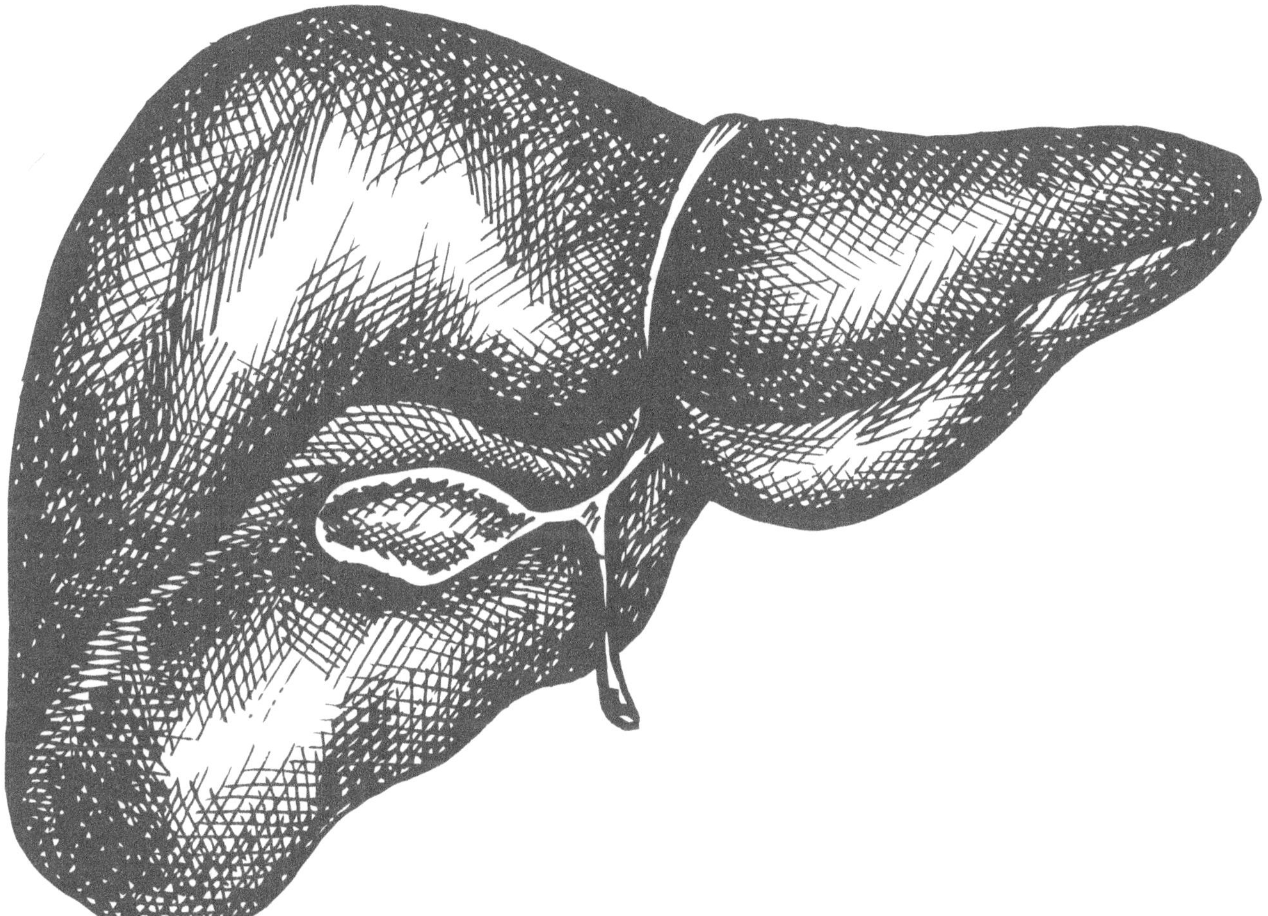

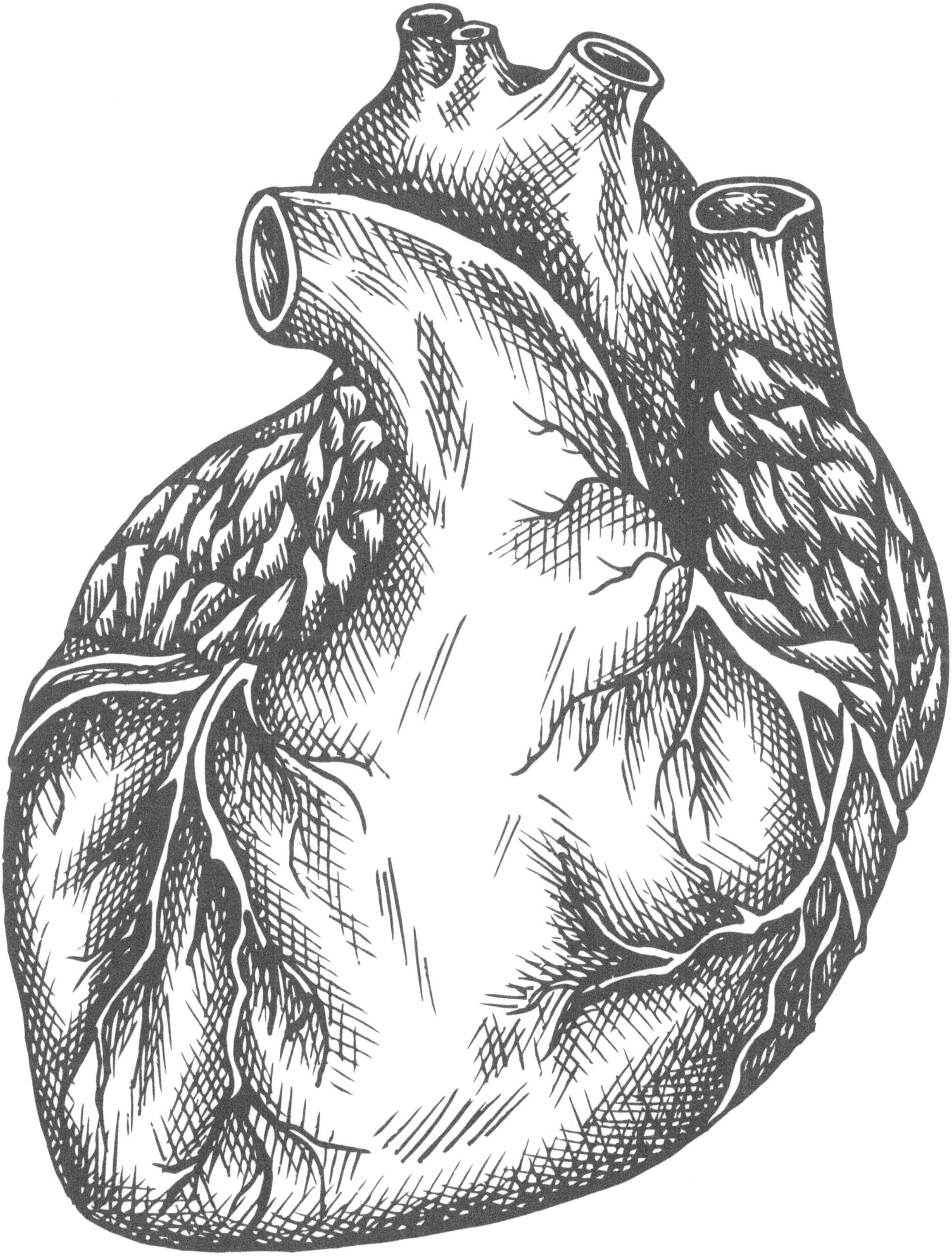

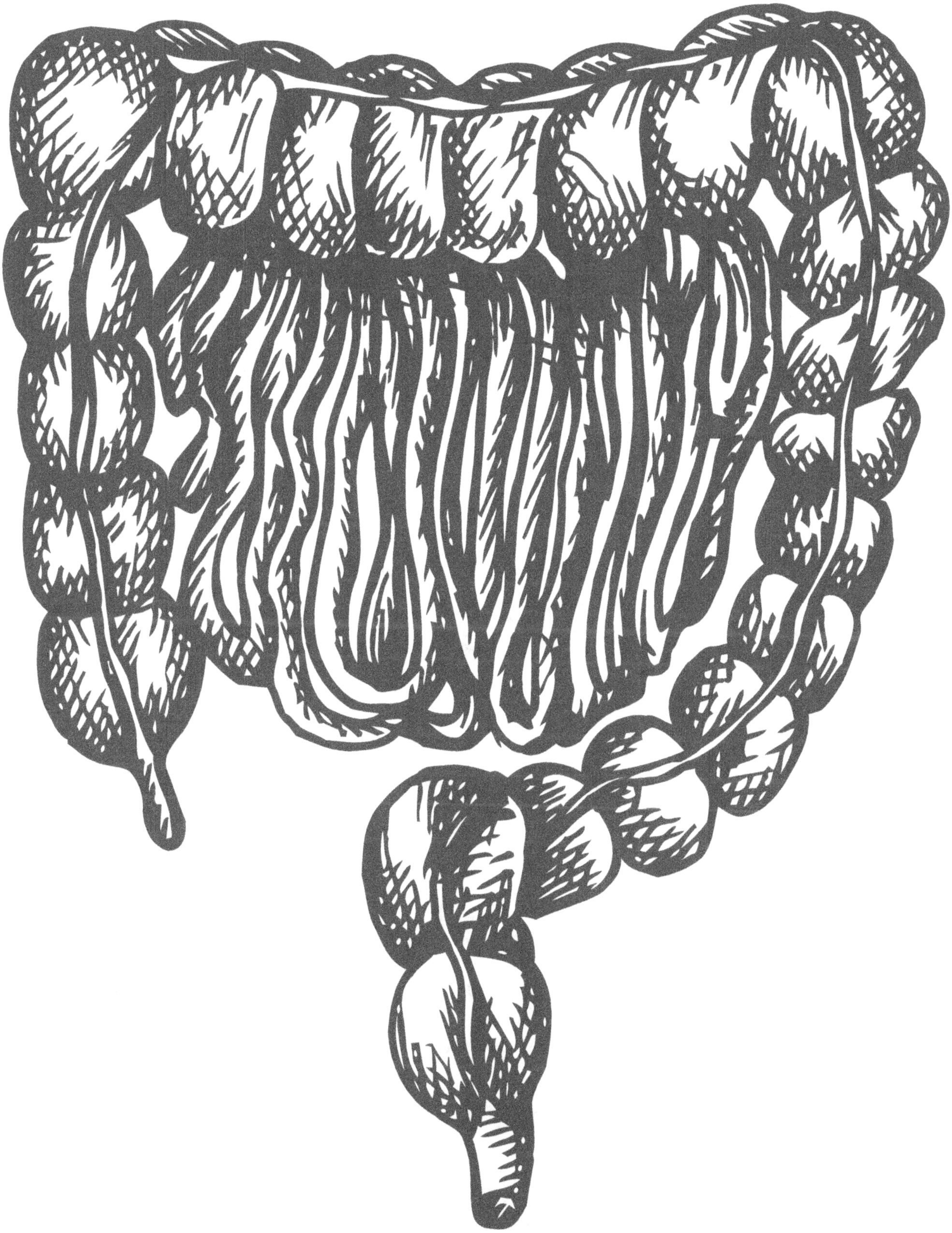

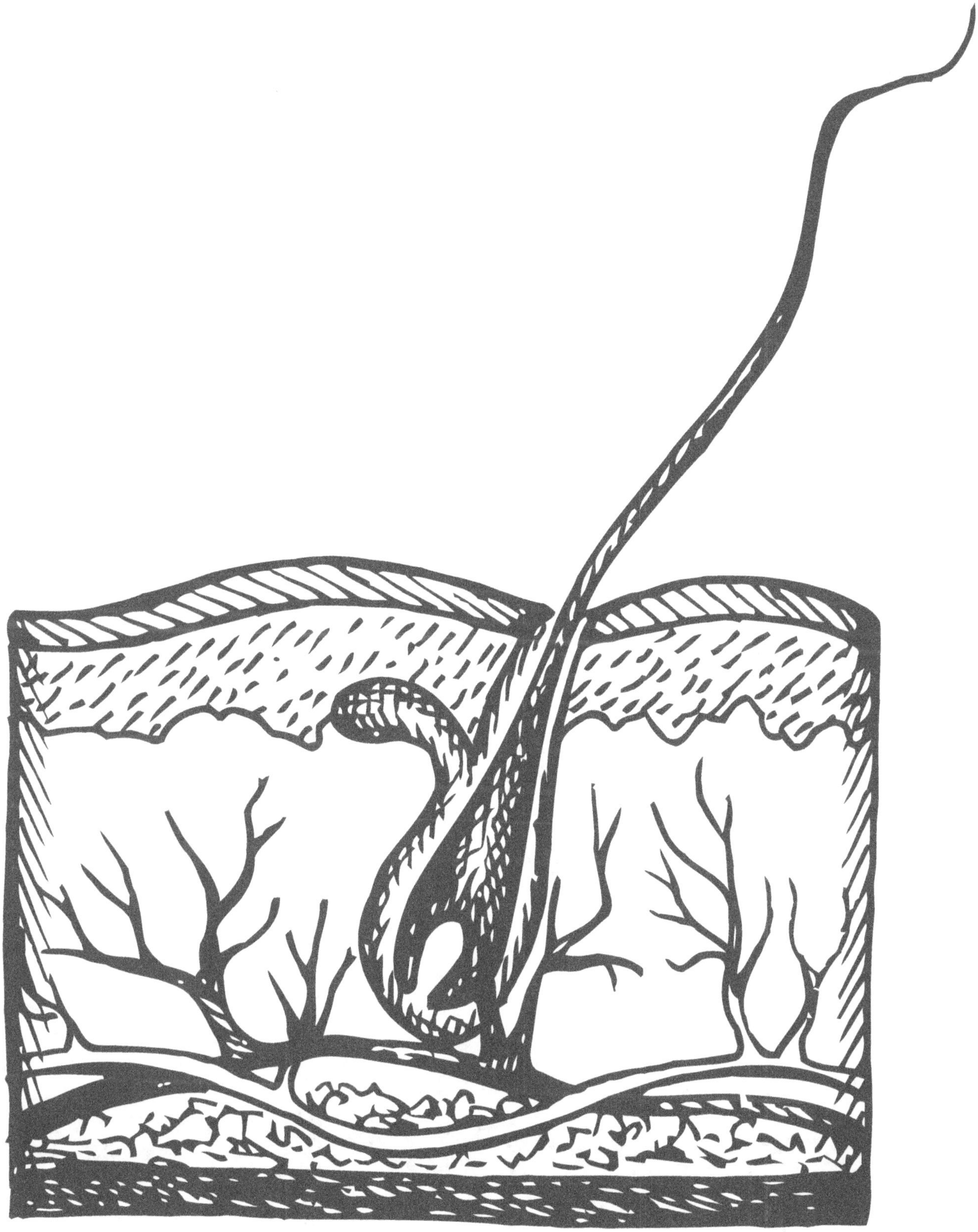

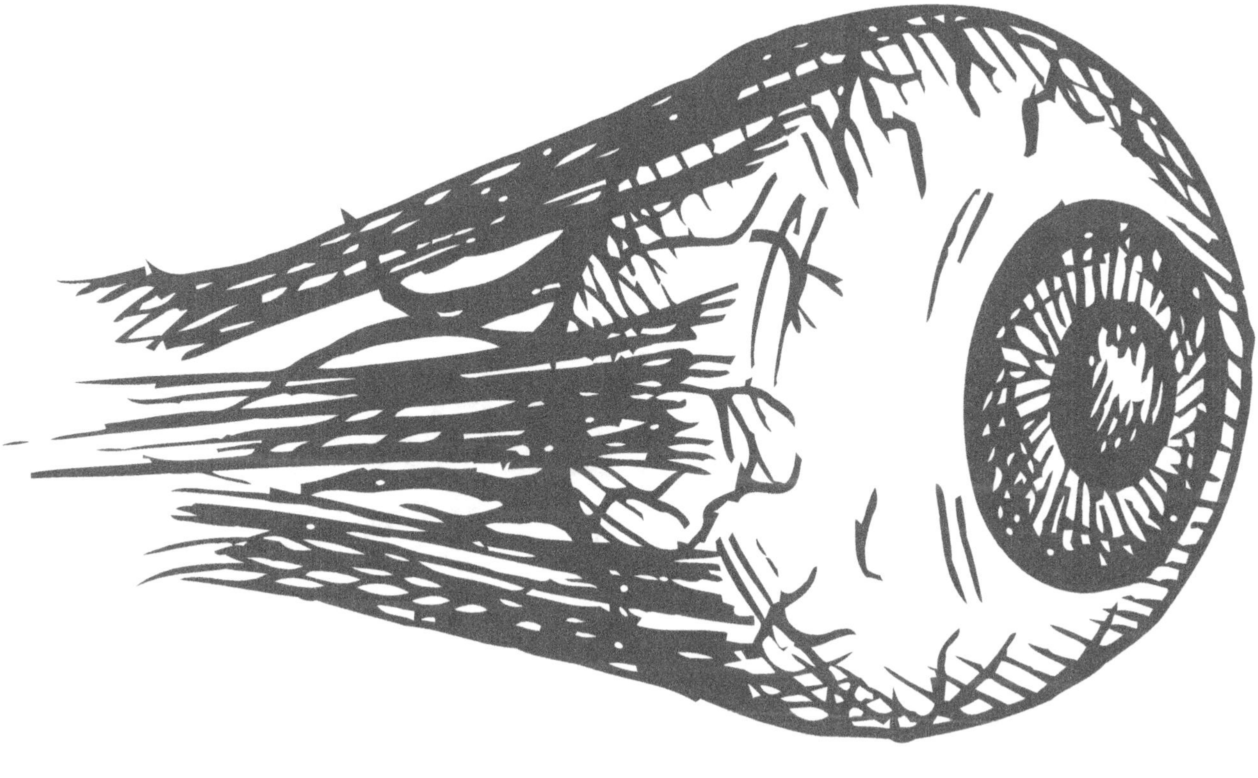

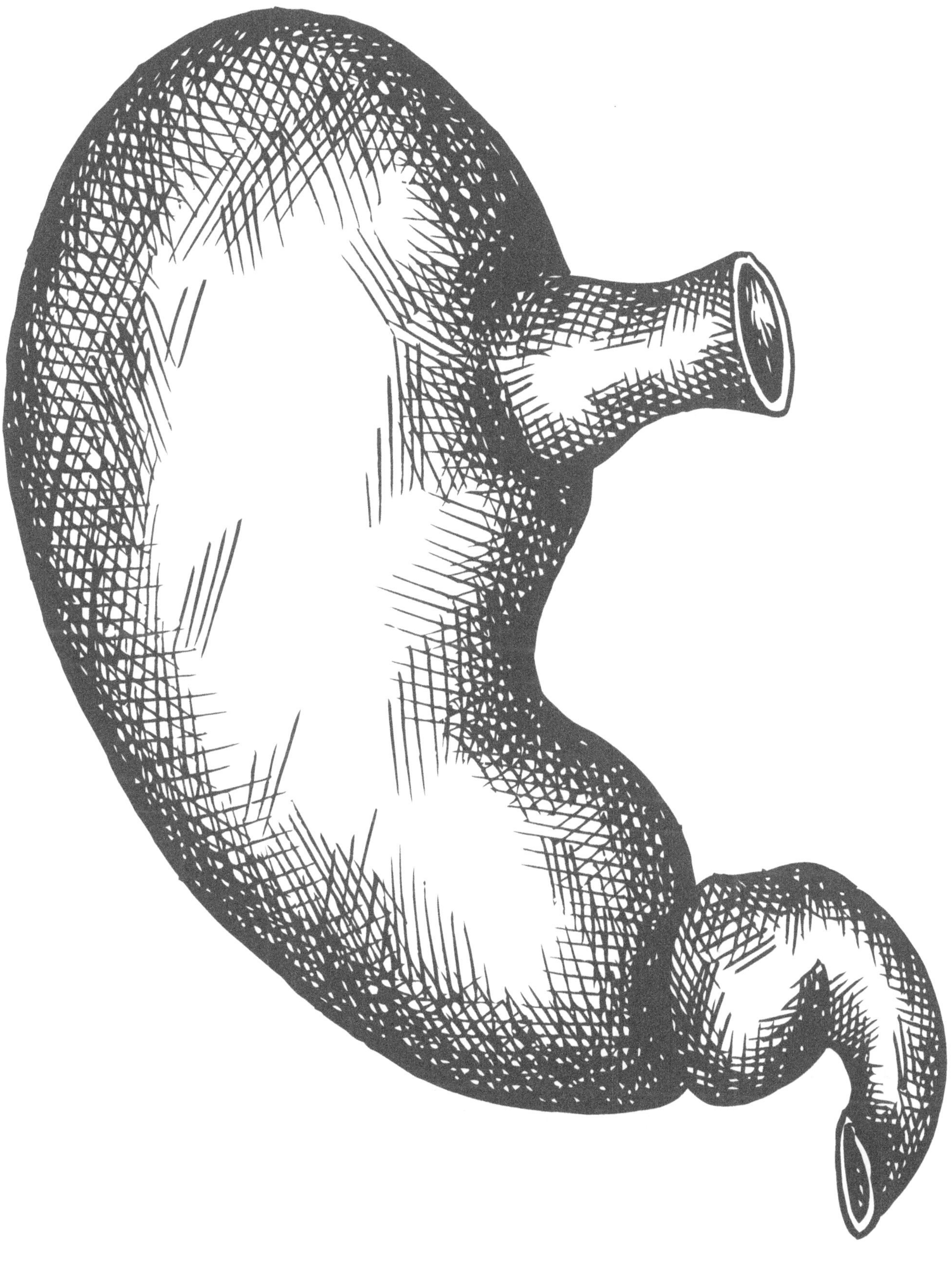

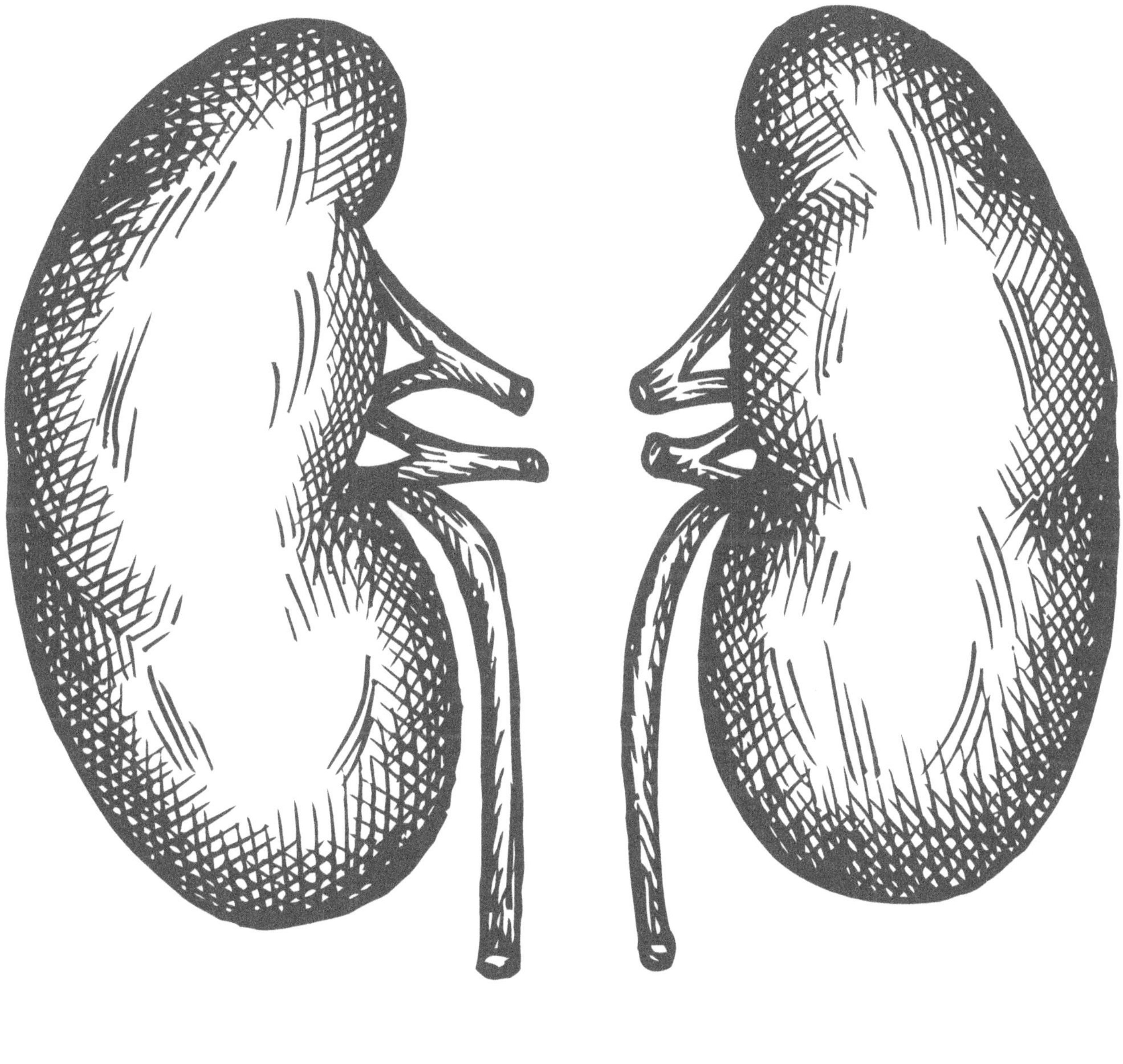

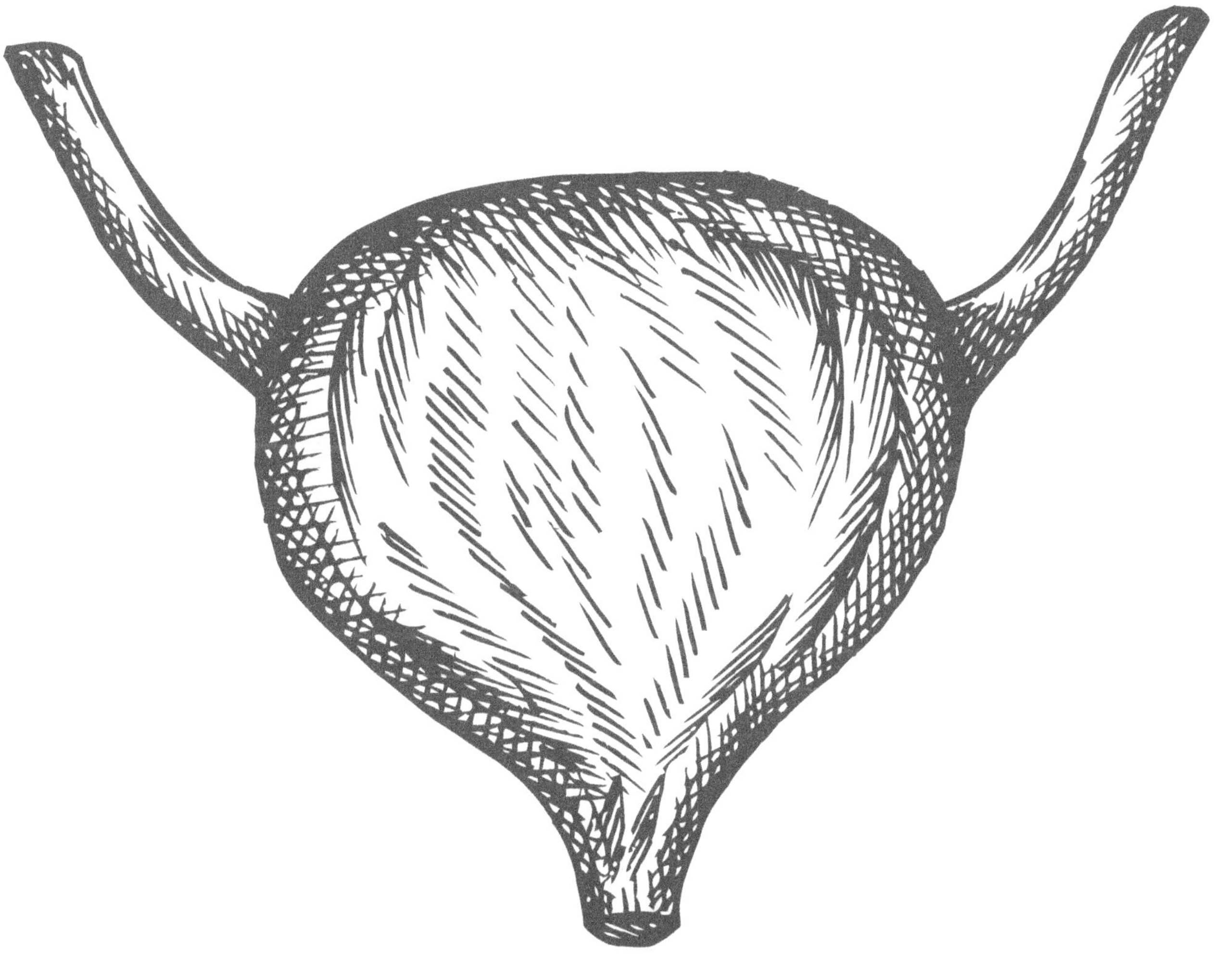

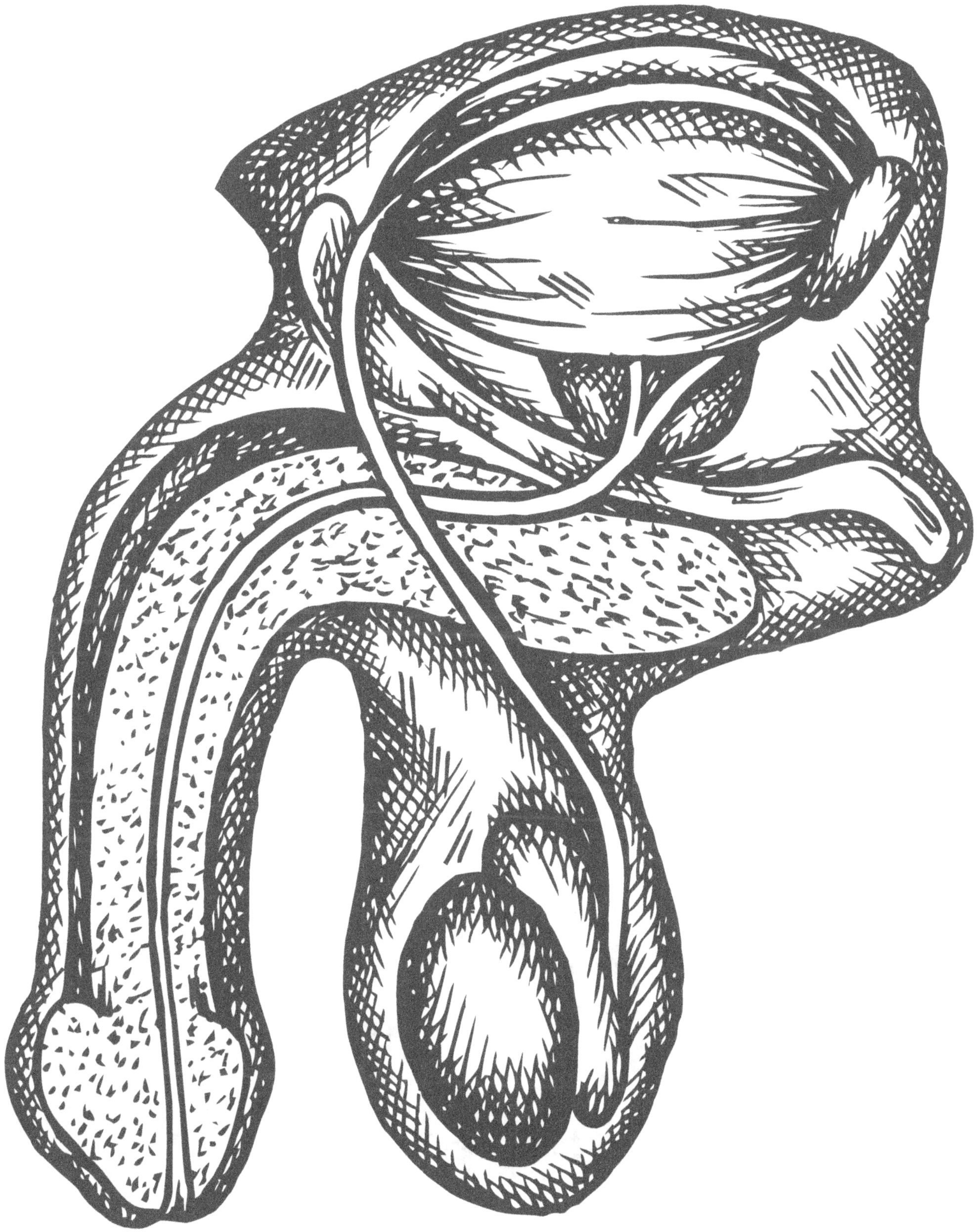

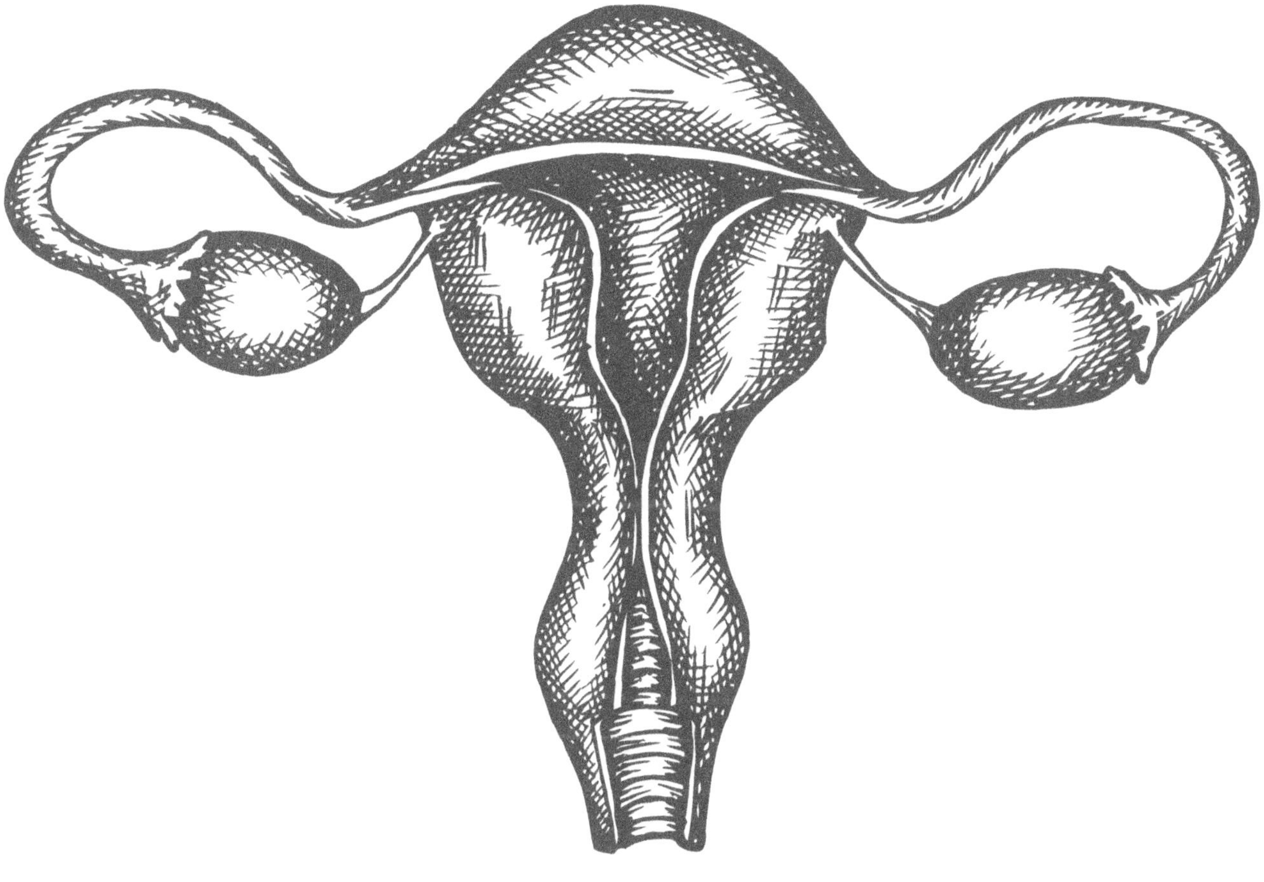

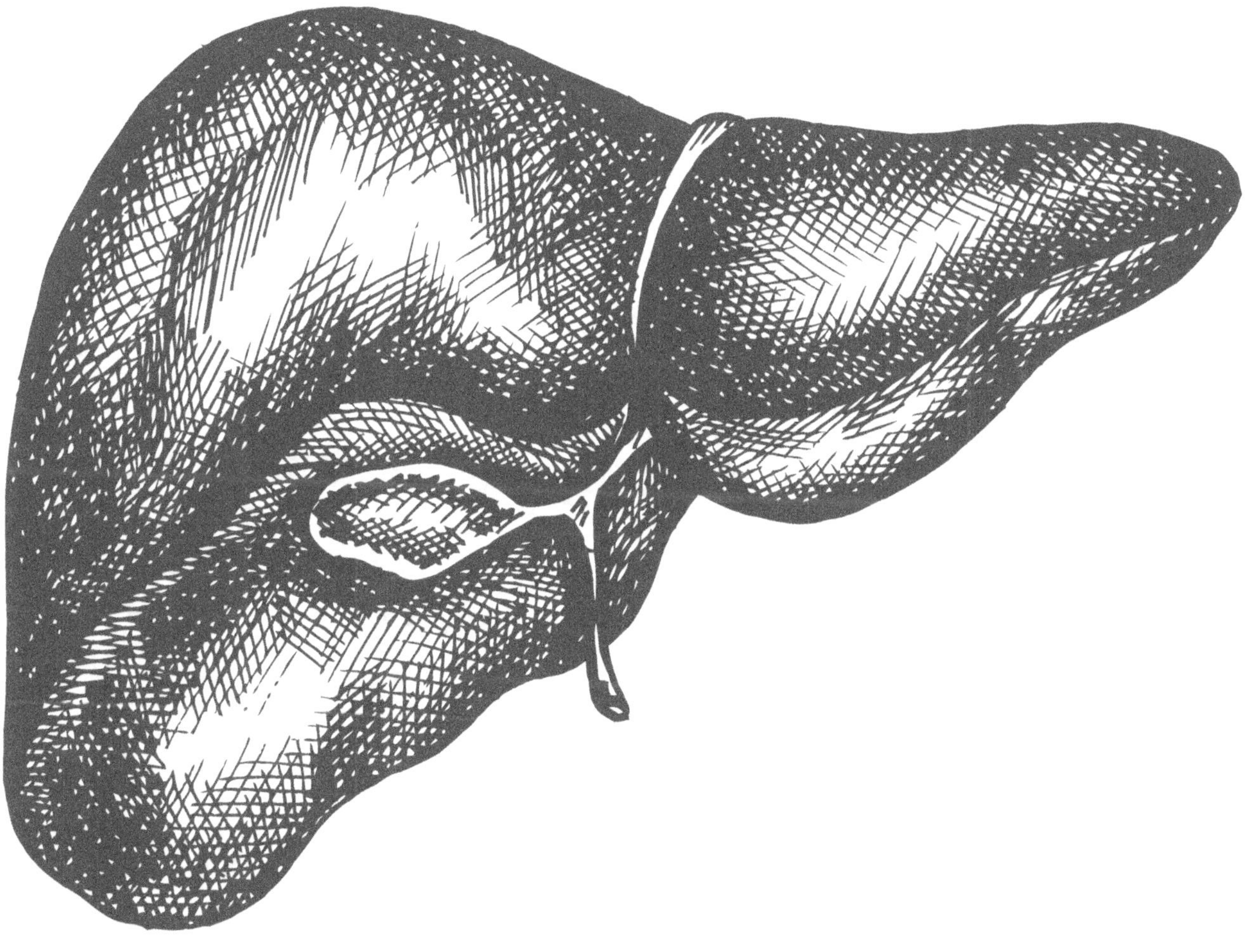

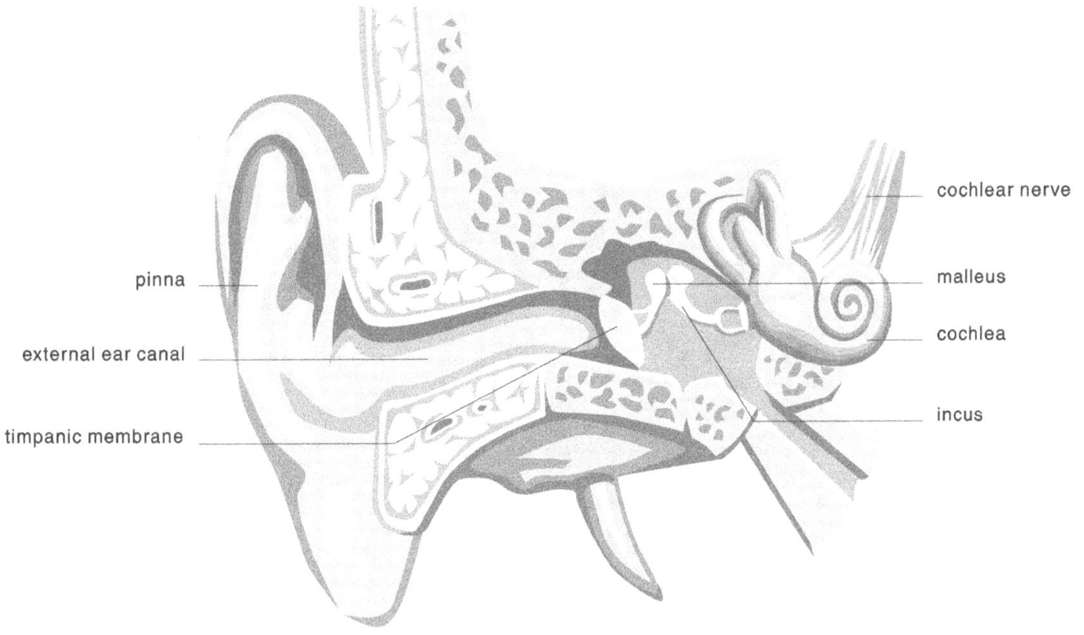
cochlear nerve
pinna
malleus
external ear canal
cochlea
incus
timpanic membrane

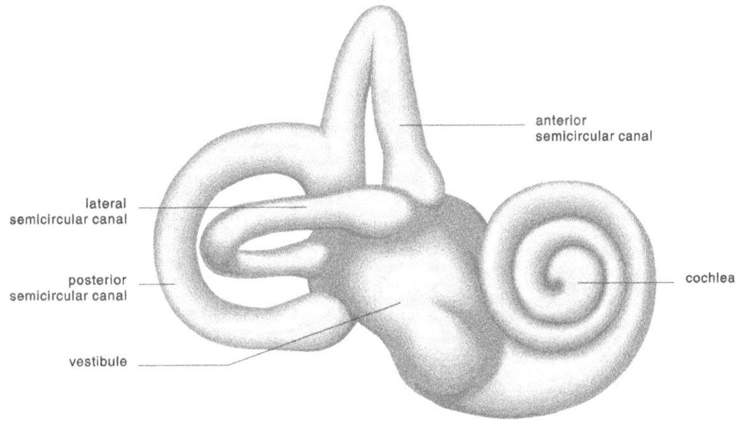
anterior
semicircular canal
lateral
semicircular canal
cochlea
posterior
semicircular canal
vestibule

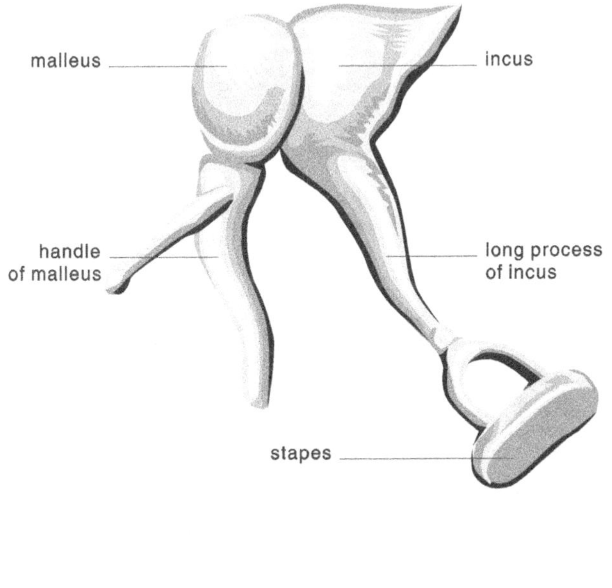
malleus
incus
handle
of malleus
long process
of incus
stapes

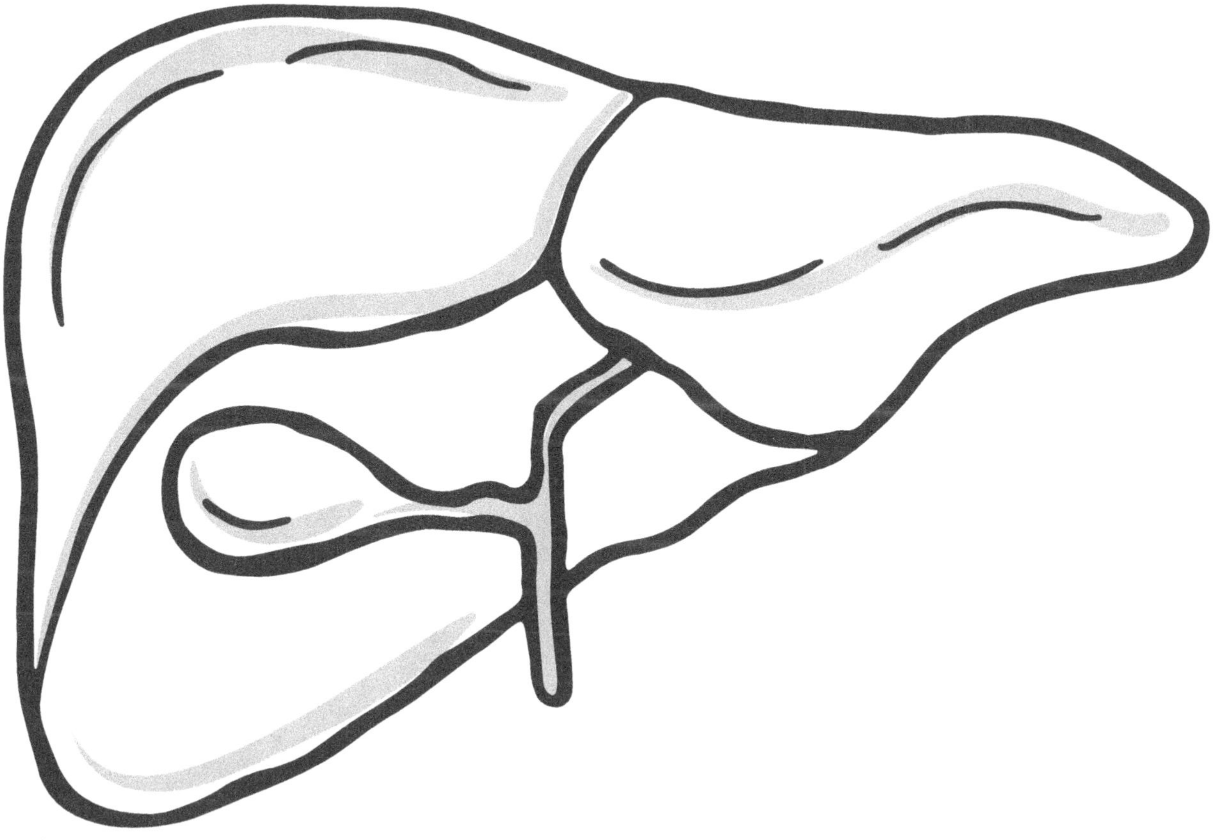

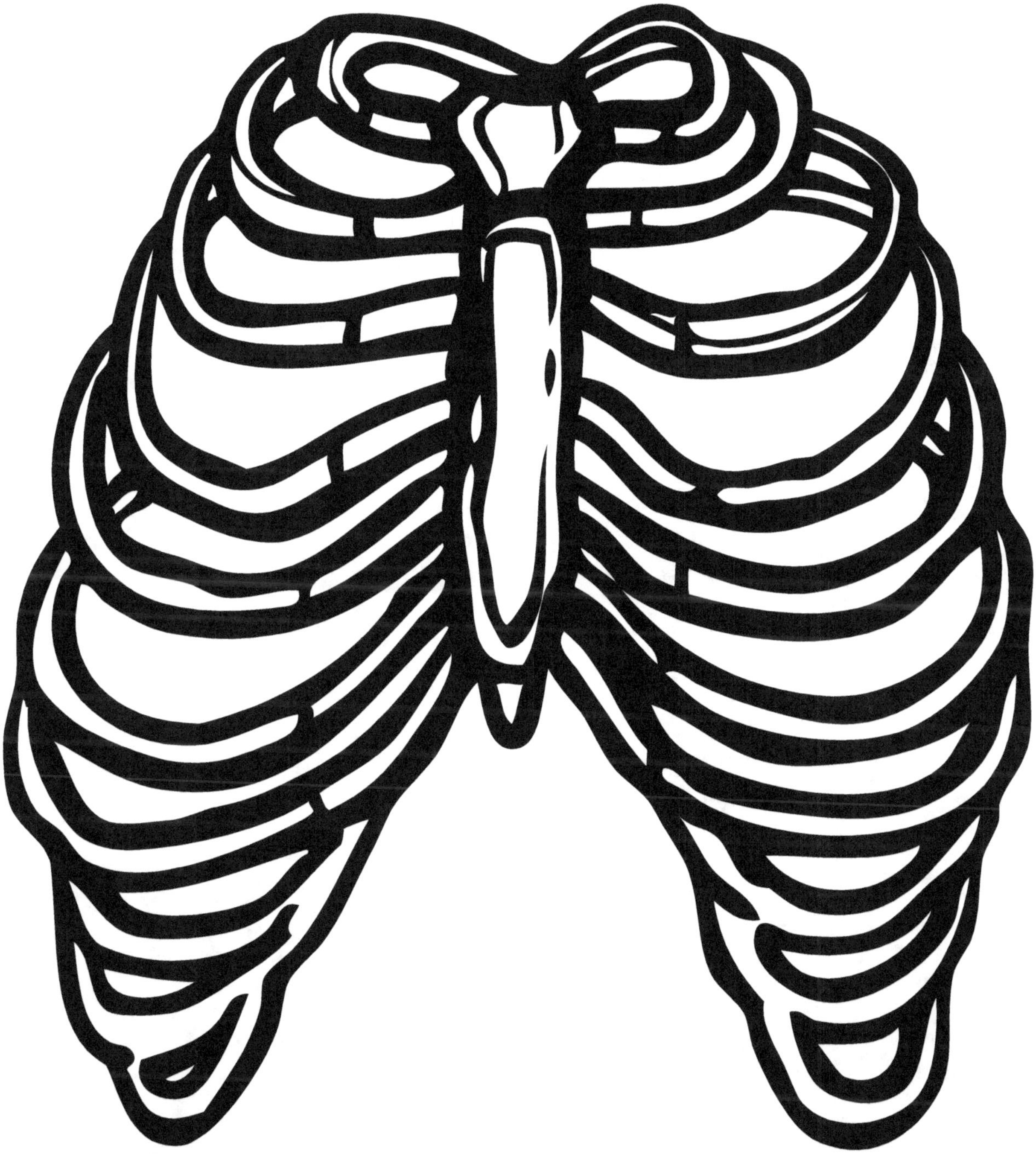

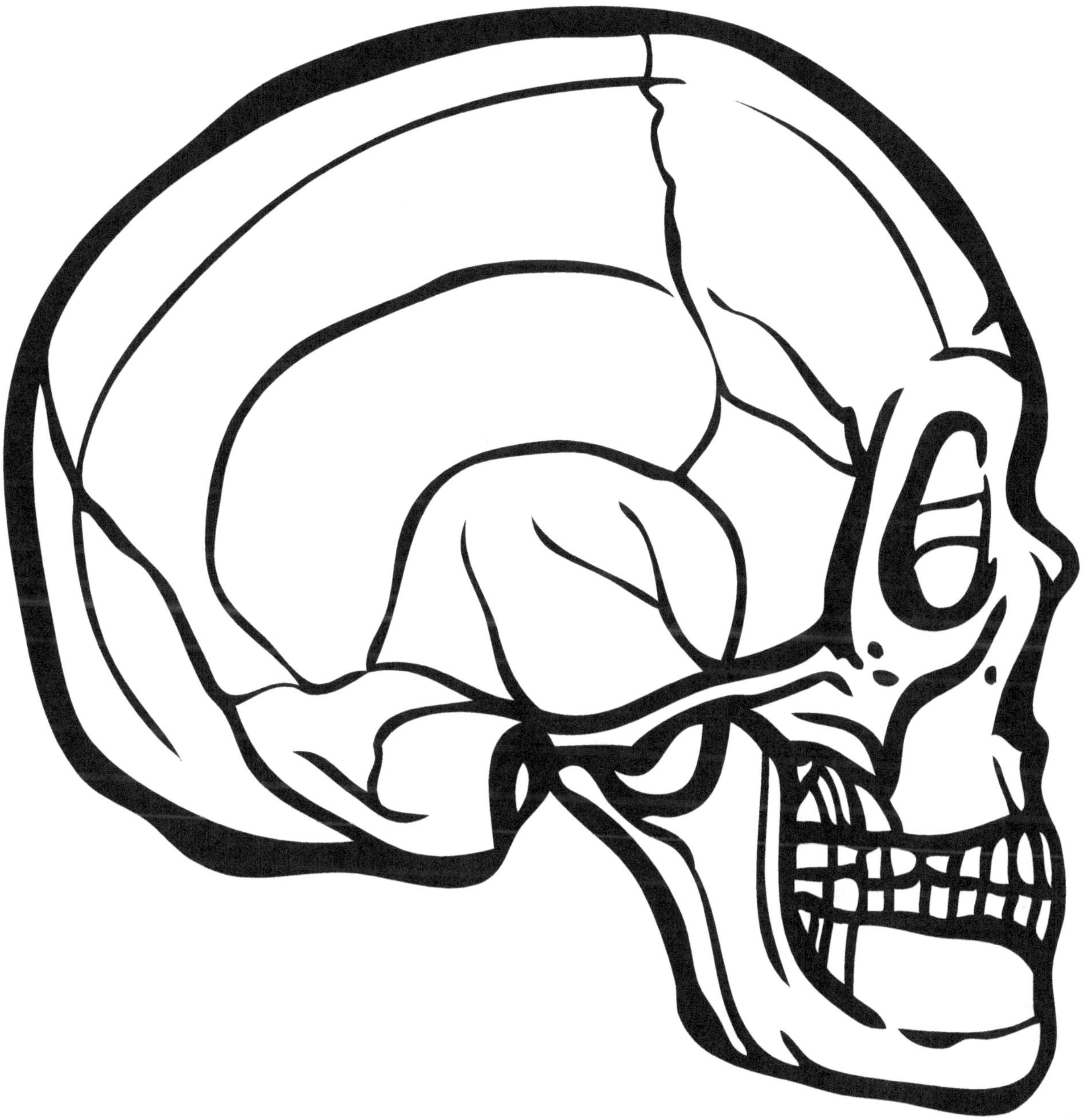

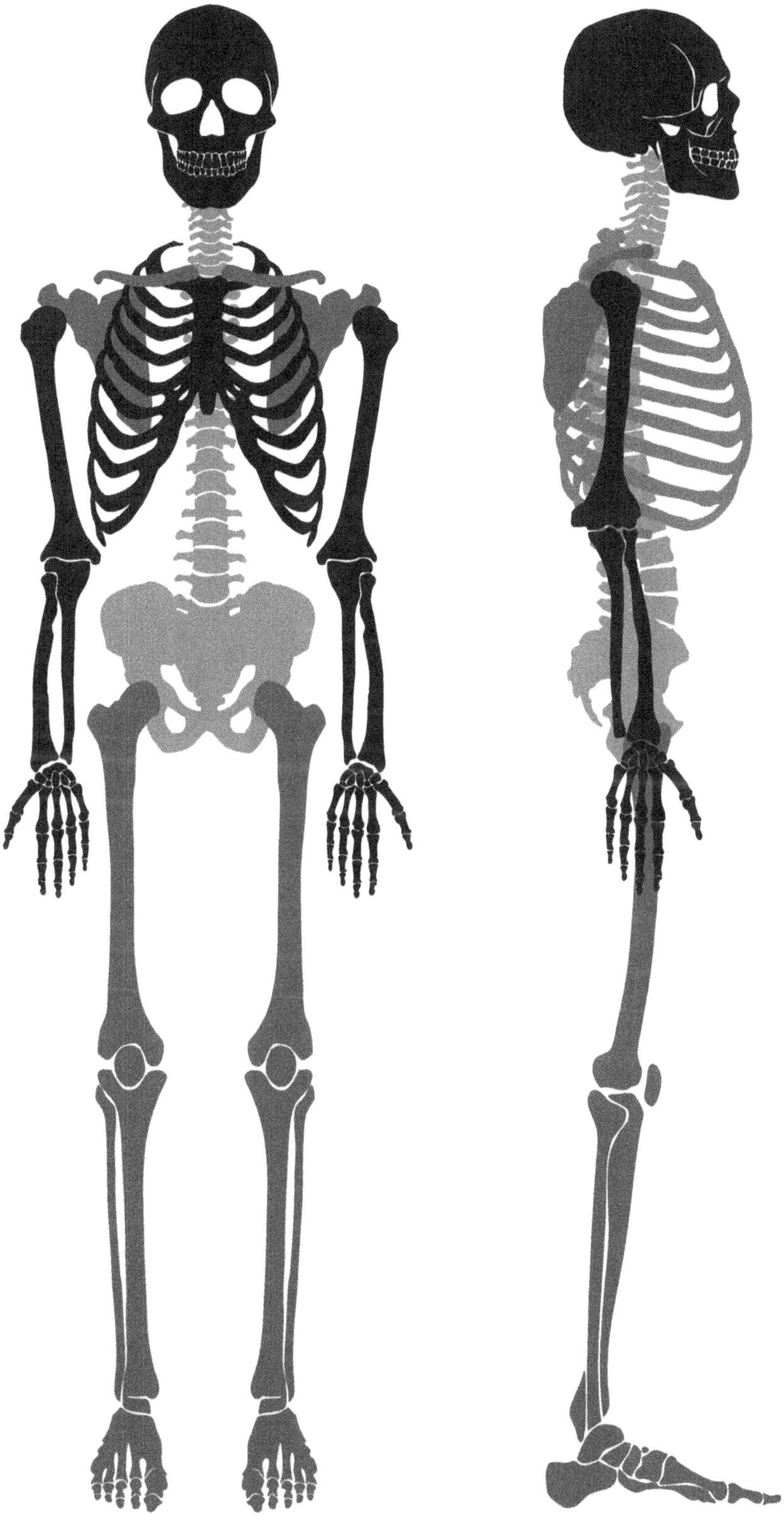

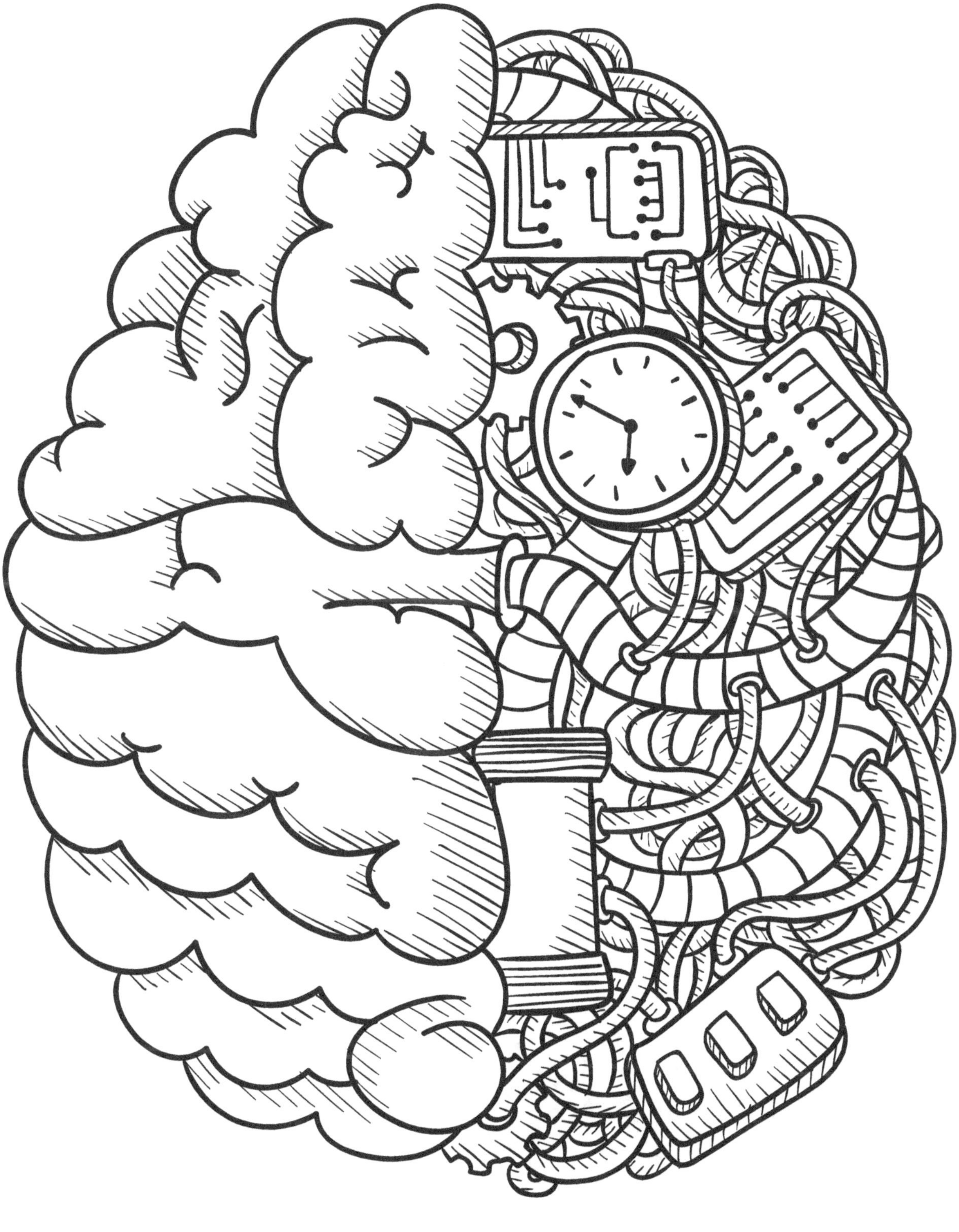

www.ingramcontent.com/pod-product-compliance
Lightning Source LLC
Chambersburg PA
CBHW081543220526
45467CB00010B/3304
* 9 7 8 1 7 0 4 9 7 4 2 2 4 *